A STEVEN SPIELBERG FILM

INDIANA J

and the
KINGDOM OF
THE CRYSTAL SKULL ™

Alfred Publishing Co., Inc.
16320 Roscoe Blvd., Suite 100
P.O. Box 10003
Van Nuys, CA 91410-0003
alfred.com

ISBN-10: 0-7390-5572-0
ISBN-13: 978-0-7390-5572-4

CONTENTS

RAIDERS MARCH

Music by
JOHN WILLIAMS

March (♩ = 120)

Raiders March - 4 - 1
31379

4

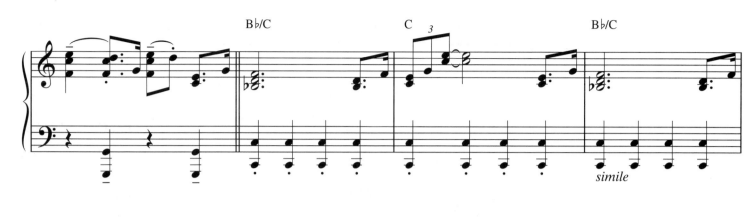

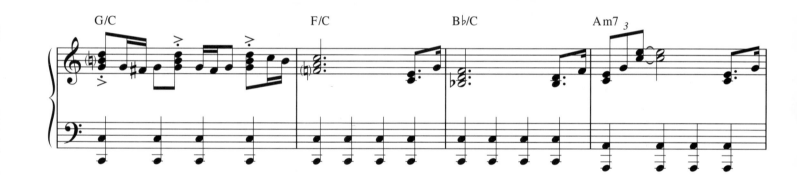

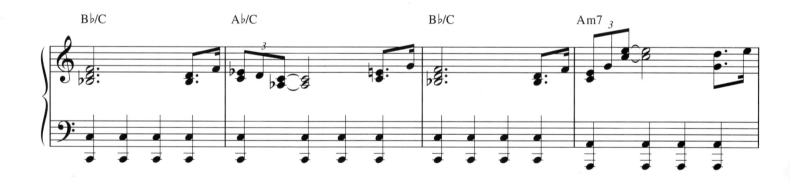

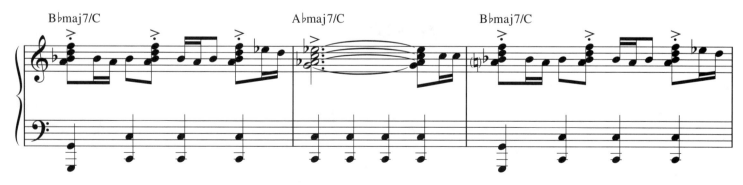

MARION'S THEME
(as featured in RAIDERS MARCH)

Music by
JOHN WILLIAMS

Moderately slow

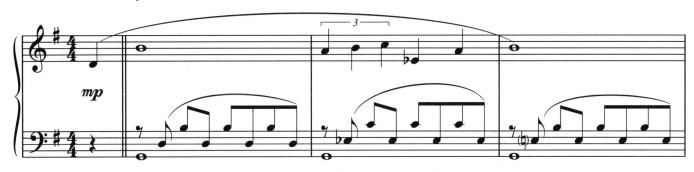

Marion's Theme - 2 - 1
31379

8

THE CRYSTAL SPELL

Music by
JOHN WILLIAMS

Moderately slow ($\quarternote$ = 76)

(with pedal)

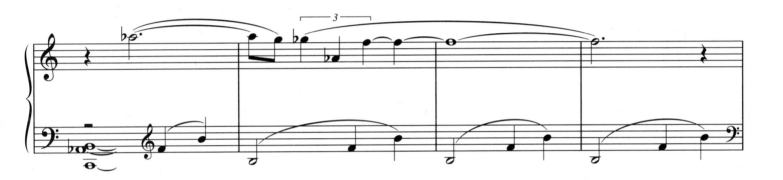

THE ADVENTURES OF MUTT

Music by
JOHN WILLIAMS

Moderately bright (♩ = 144 – 152)

The Adventures of Mutt - 5 - 1
31379

IRINA'S THEME

Music by
JOHN WILLIAMS

Moderato, espressivo (♩ = 72)

THE JOURNEY TO AKATOR

Music by
JOHN WILLIAMS